Fighting for Gold

The 10 Keys to Being a Successful Athlete

Emma Araish
10 years old

Fighting for Gold: The 10 Keys to Being a Successful Athlete
www.FightingForGold.com
Copyright © 2020 Emma Araish

ISBN: 978-1-77277-396-5

All rights reserved. No portion of this book may be reproduced mechanically, electronically, or by any other means, including photocopying, without permission of the publisher or author except in the case of brief quotations embodied in critical articles and reviews. It is illegal to copy this book, post it to a website, or distribute it by any other means without permission from the publisher or author.

Limits of Liability and Disclaimer of Warranty
The author and publisher shall not be liable for your misuse of the enclosed material. This book is strictly for informational and educational purposes only.

Warning – Disclaimer
The purpose of this book is to educate and entertain. The author and/or publisher do not guarantee that anyone following these techniques, suggestions, tips, ideas, or strategies will become successful. The author and/or publisher shall have neither liability nor responsibility to anyone with respect to any loss or damage caused, or alleged to be caused, directly or indirectly by the information contained in this book.

Medical Disclaimer
The medical or health information in this book is provided as an information resource only and is not to be used or relied on for any diagnostic or treatment purposes. This information is not intended to be patient education, does not create any patient-physician relationship, and should not be used as a substitute for professional diagnosis and treatment.

Publisher
10-10-10 Publishing
Markham, ON   Canada

Printed in Canada and the United States of America

Table of Contents

Dedication v
Foreword vii
Acknowledgements ix

Chapter 1: Introduction 1
Chapter 2: My Beginnings 7
Chapter 3: Doing What You Love 15
Chapter 4: Finding the Right Coach 21
Chapter 5: Building a Support System 29
Chapter 6: Sleeping Well 37
Chapter 7: Eating Well 43
Chapter 8: Making Sacrifices 49
Chapter 9: Having the Right Equipment 55
Chapter 10: Looking Up to Role Models 63
Chapter 11: Having the Right Mindset 69
Chapter 12: Performing in School 77
Chapter 13: Where I Am Now 83

About the Author 91

I dedicate this book to all young athletes and aspiring athletes. I hope this book will provide you with information that will help you throughout your career.

Foreword

Fighting for Gold: The 10 Keys to Being a Successful Athlete will make you realize how much work and sacrifice is involved in becoming an accomplished athlete. Not only does author Emma Araish describe important keys to flourishing as a competitor, but she also adds valuable and concrete examples from her figure skating experience. If you incorporate Emma's teachings into your daily routine, not only will you undoubtedly improve as an athlete, but you will surely become more successful in life.

Emma is a young and very successful figure skater whose track record demonstrates it. She began competing at 6 years old and has continuously improved on her provincial rankings. Emma doesn't only excel on the ice, but she also performs well in the classroom. She understands that keeping her grades up will allow her to spend more time pursuing her passion.

Do you have talent in your sport but wonder why you are not as successful as you would like? Do you wish you could take your talent to the next level? Have you been struggling to be on top in your sport? Then this book is a must read.

Emma's athletic experience has positioned her to provide you with multiple keys to becoming more successful in your sport, from eating well and sleeping well to having the right mindset and role models. Her book will serve as a guide, and will reveal the secrets to becoming a more successful athlete. Simply follow Emma's keys and you will surely begin your rise to the top.

Happy reading!

Kaetlyn Osmond
Figure Skating World Champion

Acknowledgements

Gabriel Araish. Daddy, thank you for supporting me while writing this book. I am grateful for all the time you have given me and my sport, for always bringing my spirits up and encouraging me. For the past few years, you have brought me to the rink on a daily basis, watched me skate and helped me stay focused. I am very lucky to have you as a daddy. I love you.

Marie-Andrée Dupuis. Thank you for always supporting me. I am grateful for your non-stop positive attitude. You never let me quit. Even in life, you always know what to say and after your pep talks, I always know what to do. You lived a life where you had to depend on yourself. You had to work so hard to achieve everything you have, and I admire you for that. I love you.

William Araish. Little brother, thank you for being such a ball of joy. I am grateful for you always cheering for me. I love hearing you scream my name when I get on the ice. Thank you for being who you are; just seeing you smile makes me happy, and when I don't have time before school to hug you my heart is broken. I love you.

Caroline Scalzo. Thank you for being such a great coach and influence in my life. I have learned and continue to learn so much from you. You helped me discover my passion and I'll always be grateful for that.

Annie Barabé. Thank you for the opportunity to skate with some of the best coaches in the province. I am grateful for your trust and confidence in me.

Kaetlyn Osmond. Thank you for being a role model for me. I am grateful for having had the opportunity to learn as I watched you skate. I love your smile and performances.

Eladj Balde. Thank you for taking time out of your day to teach everyone dance routines and keep us moving. You have a mission to make figure skating available to anyone who wants to skate. I am so grateful for all your help and for what you bring to this beautiful sport.

Myriame Laroche. Thank you for always encouraging me, coaching me and being present for my competitions. I am grateful for the time you have invested in me, and for your contributions to this book.

Marc Lemay. Thank you being an amazing athletic therapist, taking care of my body and taking the time to explain the mechanics of my body, my pains and how to treat and prevent injuries. I am grateful to have you as part of my support system.

Julie Marcotte. Thank you for being a great choreographer. I love your choreographies. Skaters that have their routines prepared by you are very lucky and I hope that, one day, I am privileged enough to skate on one of your performances.

CPA L'oiseau bleu de Mascouche. Thank you for welcoming me into your club and making me feel at home. I am proud to represent you every time I skate.

Steve Laframboise. Thank you for providing a place where skaters can find the right equipment to be able to perform. I am grateful for all that you do for me and the figure skating community.

Diane Nardo. Thank you for always being nice to me when I come into the skating store. I am grateful for you always making sure I have the right equipment, especially skates.

Raymond Aaron. Thank you for teaching me everything I know, like singing the alphabet backwards. I am grateful for the time you took to teach a little girl like me. I am still working on speaking well but, thanks to you, I know more than most people.

Daniela Donoso Paredes and **Waqas Chaudhry.** Thank you for being so helpful. This book would not have been completed without your guidance. I am so grateful for your time and generosity.

Tom Brady. Thank you for being a model of hard work and consistency. I learned a lot from the way you approach and prepare for each game. You had a dream and you achieved it, and I am willing to follow your footsteps to succeed in my sport.

Kobe Bryant†. Thank you for being a role model to me. I know we practice a different sport but there is one thing I really learned from you. If you work hard and put your mind to it, you can achieve anything. You were a great help in my career without even knowing it, and I am grateful for that.

Family

Edgar Araish, Nariman Araish, Marc Araish, Maria Varano, Leila Mia Araish, Lara Grace Araish, Claire Blondin, Catherine Blondin, René Dupuis, Johanne Champagne, Pierre Chalifoux, Annick Lussier, Nicolas Cournoyer, Florence Cournoyer, Zac Chalifoux.

Gabriel Araiche†, Alice Araiche†, Issa Araiche†, Diane Araiche, Denise Araiche, Gabriel I. Araiche, Lisa Araiche, Daniel Araiche, Julia Araiche, James Araiche, Rima Mair, Andrew Mair, Charles Mair, Nicole Mair Hala Mair, Leila Bettio, Gabriel Bettio, Danielle Bettio, Veronica Bettio, Danielle Araiche, Richard Araish, Diana Araish, Gabriel R. Araish, Tracey Darke, Richie Araish, Yasmeen Araish, Alice Martone, Franco Martone, Christian Martone, Julian Martone, Vincent Martone, Jackie Yovanovski, Lupcho Yovanovski, Ashley Yovanovski, Tiffany Yovanovski, Leila Marroum, François Marroum, Rania Iaccino, Serge Iaccino, Tania Bernardini, Roly Bernardini, Lucas Bernardini, Jessica Bernardini, Dinah Pitassio, Joe Pitassio, Paul Pitassio, Ramzi Marroum, Marlène Marroum, Tina Marroum, Bryan Kingston, Karen Blakey, Ian Blakey.

Charles-Henri Blondin†, Rita Lamy†, Jacques Blondin, Louise Blondin, Guy Blondin, Claire Rémillard Blondin, Nicole Blondin, Micheline Blondin†, Isabelle Tougas, Stéphane Gratton, Vincent Gratton, Laurie Gratton, Michelle Blondin, Eve

Fighting for Gold

Richard, Francis Lessard, Jean Blondin, Jean-Guy Dupuis, Yvette Lafond, Alain Dupuis, Dominique Gouin, Nicole Dupuis.

Nina Chedid†, Fouad Chedid†, Sami Chedid, Aida Helou, Jad Chedid, Adam Chedid, Nicolas Chedid, Rana Estephan, Georgette Estephan, Nadine Chedid, Rony Chedid, Rola Chedid, Georges Sidawi†, Samia Sidawi, Nada Sidawi, Sharad Dudeja, Fadi Sidawi, Pascale Riel, Maxime Sidawi, Antoine Sidawi, Nabil Sidawi.

Friends

Nancy Alexander, François Archambault, Raphaëlle Archambault, Sabrina Betina, Hicham Boutamine, Lena Boutamine, Sophia Boutamine, Chantal Beaudin, Janine Beaudin, Nicole Beaudin, Ronald Beaudin, Caroline Béliveau, Léonie Bellemare, Rita Boummerhi, Gianni Cantini, Olivia Cantini, Briana Cianci, Gianni Cianci, Samia Coache-Luqman, Suzanne Cyr, Giuliano De Rose, Sofia De Rose, Annie Di Bartolomeo, Daniel Di Bartolomeo, Frank Di Bartolomeo, Franco Di Paola, Gemma Di Paola, Nadia Fallavollita, Davide Fasulo, Giuseppe Fasulo, Nicolas Fasulo, Francesco Galluccio, Annabelle Gauvin, Sophia Ivanov, Chelsey James, Maude Julien, Ann Kane, Camille Kane, France Kingsbury, Marco Kozlowski, Héloïse Lafleur, Johanne Lecavalier, Sarah Leduc, Romy Lessard, Loïk Lessard, Martin Lessard, Maria Madison Di Giovanni, Anthony Malapetsas, Ioannis Malapetsas, Melina Malapetsas, Erika Magini, Eva Magini, Cylia Marks, Chloe Mentha, Carly Milorin, Alexandra Morar, Ioana Morar, Vlad

Morar, Sandra Moretti, Victoria Nevers, Bindu Patel, Irène Pelletier, Mégane-Rose Pelletier, André Perron, Cherine Perron, Georgette Perron, Julie Perron, Philippe Perron, Elio Perciballi, Gianni Perciballi, Liana Perciballi, Francesca Petrizzo, Albina Pirillo, Elisaveta Poirier, Sabrina Polletta, Luigi Porcot, Marcello Porco, Stefano Porco, Alexia Richard, Dominique Rivest, Rose Savard-Ferguson, Roxanne Sbitti, Dino Scmrechert, Connie Screnci, Marco Screnci, Marco Screnci, Mia Screnci, Kelly-Anne St-Hilaire, Sabrina St-Hilaire, Malika Stiverne, Ally Théodat, Carl Théodat, Carlot Théodat, Imany Théodat, Nikita Théodat, Antonio Trevisonno, Robert Trevisonno, Vincenzo Trevisonno, Phoebe Winser, Annie Yan.

Coaches and Teachers

François Archambault, Maddalena Borrega, Peter Borrega, Benjamin Brisebois, Serge Champagne, Lynda Chery, Amanda D'Aloia, Charles Dion, Isabelle Dupré, Andrew Ferla-Coirazza, Josiane Fréchette, Kateri Gagnon, Julie Guindon, Caroline Hébert, Nathalie Labarre, Chantal Lefebvre, Joé Letendre, Carolyne Lozeau, Véronik Mallet, Sylvain Mallette, Isabelle Massé, Monica Nachi, Karine Nolet, Sandy Orelus, Michele Palmieri-Colatriano, Julie Paré, Mark Passaretti, Walnise Pharins, Marlène Picard, Gabriella Petrin, Sabrina Petrin, Sophie Richard, Danièle Robillard, Christina Romano, Caroline Rooney, Camille Ruest, Véronique Sigouin, Julie St-Amour, Arina Voloshenenko.

Chapter 1
Introduction

Success comes from knowing that you did your best to become the best that you are capable of becoming.
- John Wooden

In writing this book, I wanted to share the keys to being a successful athlete. Being a successful athlete does not mean you are an Olympian or a professional; it simply means you love what you do, want to keep doing it and want to be your best at it. As a young figure skater who went from skating for fun just 4 years ago to being ranked third in the province in my age group today, I have learned that there are things you can do to improve your performance and success. I believe there are 10 keys to being a successful athlete. These apply to figure skating, but can also apply to any sport, such as hockey, soccer, tennis, gymnastics and many more. Many of the 10 keys can also apply to anyone wanting to improve their life.

The 10 keys are:

- Doing what you love
- Finding the right coach
- Building a support system
- Sleeping well
- Eating well
- Making sacrifices
- Having the right equipment

- Looking up to role models
- Having the right mindset
- Performing in school

I hope you enjoy reading this book as much as I enjoyed writing it.

Happy reading!

Emma

Chapter 2
My Beginnings

Sports do not build character. They reveal it.
- Heywood Broun

Before I talk about the 10 keys to being a successful athlete, I would like to talk about how it all started for me. I remember being almost 4 years old. I was still at daycare and enjoying birthday parties, eating cake, doing arts and crafts, and I was learning how to read with my mommy. I was also excited to meet my little brother because my mommy was pregnant. One day, my parents told me it was my first day of skating lessons. On the way to the ice rink, I was so excited and looking forward to it. Even if I was not too sure what skating was about. I had never skated before, but it sounded fun.

Once at the ice rink, I put my skates on for the first time. My skates were very small, white on the outside with a pink cushion on the inside. I was excited to go on the ice; it was beautiful, white and shiny like winter. As you can imagine, once I put my two feet on the ice, I fell right away. I started crying and got scared. I did not want to skate anymore; it hurt, and I cried and cried and cried. My parents told me that I cried for the first 4 weeks, and did not want to get on the ice. My parents continued to bring me and said to never quit even if it is hard. The teachers were nice, and the first thing they taught me was how to get up on my own, which was good because all I did was fall. Once I learned how to balance on my two skates, I started to enjoy skating.

Skate Canada has a development program with six steps. Every time I completed a step, I would receive a badge. To get a badge, I had to achieve certain skating elements as well as certain levels of agility and balance. I had to achieve five badges in order to be considered experienced enough to remove my helmet, which was very exciting. After my first year, I got my first badge and I was very happy. The other girls already had badges on their skirts and now, I had my own to decorate my skirt.

I continued the group classes until I was 5 years old. Then, my parents were told I was selected to participate in a development program at the club. I didn't know what that meant, but I did receive my second badge, and I got to wear a red skirt instead of a blue one, so I was really happy because it was pretty. The red skirt meant that I was part of the development program. My parents were surprised that I was selected; they did not expect it as I was nowhere near the best skater on the ice. My parents then explained to me that this was a development program for skaters who met certain age and level criteria.

As much as I enjoyed getting the badges, my favorite skating moment was always the end of year show. I loved it because I got to show my parents and my family what I had worked on during the year. I also got to wear pretty costumes and makeup. My daddy was not thrilled about this. The first time I put some makeup on, my lipstick was all over my mouth. I looked like a clown but I was so happy.

That's how it all started. I knew I had found something I loved to do; I had found my passion. I have now been skating for nearly 5 years and although I still have a lot of work to do to reach my dreams, I want to share with you the 10 keys that have helped me become more successful in my sport.

Chapter 3
Doing What You Love

The size of your success is measured by the strength of your desire; the size of your dream; and how you handle disappointment along the way.
– Robert Kiyosaki

The first and most important key to being a successful athlete is doing what you love. Of course, this will apply to anything in life, but this book is about sports. If you wake up in the morning and you are not super excited to go to practice your sport, then it will be very difficult to be very good at it. If you know what you love, consider yourself very lucky, because not everyone finds what they love in life. If the first thing you think about when you wake up is practicing your sport, then that is probably your passion. If you would rather practice your sport than watch television or hang out with your friends, then that is definitely your passion.

Let me tell you about how I found out figure skating was my passion. My parents made me play soccer, take swimming lessons, and dance. For all those sports, I sometimes did not feel like going, especially soccer, and if my parents said that I would miss swimming or dance class because we had to go somewhere else, I never really cared. Then, my parents decided to put me in figure skating. As mentioned in the "My Beginnings" chapter, I actually did not like it at all for the first 4 lessons and I cried all the time. But then, once I was able to stand up and skate, I fell in love with it. I was looking forward to my parents driving me to the rink. I was so excited that when I got to skating, my daddy put my skates on but I put my helmet and my gloves on to save some time. I got ready, and when I went on the ice, I had a lot of fun because I was actually learning and enjoying gliding on the ice.

Another way to know if you love what you are practicing is if you still love it when it gets harder. If you are willing to work harder and harder when it gets difficult, then you really know you love it. If you keep trying even when you fail, that is another sign that you love what you are doing. When it gets harder for me, I push myself. I do not give up and I practice even more.

I know what my passion is. Do you know what yours is? I really hope my experience with figure skating will help you find your passion. If you still have not found your love for a sport, then I encourage you to keep trying new sports until you do. There is nothing more fun than doing what you love every day.

Chapter 4
Finding the Right Coach

The difference between a successful person and others is not a lack of strength, not a lack of knowledge, but rather a lack of will.
– Vince Lombardi

The second key to being a successful athlete is to make sure you have the right coach. I want to share with you my experience. I was 6 years old when I first got a private coach, just before the fall season. The reason I got a private coach is because I had a hard time bending my ankles and knees, which is super important to gain speed in skating. My first coach was nice. She taught me how to bend my knees and glide. At the end of each lesson she would have me race as fast as I could and beat my previous time. She did that to see if I was bending my knees and getting faster. I was, but not that much.

One of my friends at skating had skated over the summer and when she came back for the fall season, she had no more helmet. She had passed all her steps and she had gotten so much better. My parents spoke to her mom and found out she had skated all summer with my red skirt coach. They decided to change my coach, and have her coach me too. She was much stricter than my first coach; she corrected my mistakes, she did not let me fool around and she really wanted me to focus. She even got a little upset sometimes when I was not listening, but I was happy to have a coach who corrected my mistakes so I could get better and improve my technique.

With my new coach, I started to practice the first jumps that you learn in skating: Waltz Jump and Salchow. I also learned my cross-cuts, how to glide and do airplanes, also called Arabesque. It made me fall in love with the sport even more. After a few months with my new coach, I had gotten all my badges and then, one day, my coach told me I was ready to take off my helmet, so I did. She then had me show my daddy my airplanes without my helmet. I was really excited, but I think my daddy was terrified.

My coach also taught me about hard work. Every time I fell, my coach said "Come on, we will do it again and fix your mistakes." She would do that until I got it right at least 3 times in a row. That was really good because at the same time, she made me practice my consistency and to never give up. Having the right coach is important. This means having a coach that will support you, and tell you your mistakes so you can fix them to make you better. The way I improved with my coach was amazing, I went from skating for fun to a competitive level called "Sans Limites." It is a level in Quebec where you have no limits on the elements you include in your program, but also have elements that must be included in the program. This all happened in about 4 months.

I still skate with the same coach because she is still the right coach for me, and she continues to push me to get even better. I also work with other coaches because they have different expertise and strengths. I work with coaches that have a lot of experience in skating skills and dance, who teach me how to perform on the ice, and correct my movements and posture. I also practice my jumps with a coach that uses a harness, and my spins with a coach that excels in that technique. To surround myself with the best coaches, I changed training centers about a year ago. The new center is much further distance-wise than the previous one, but it has helped me improve a lot because of the quality of the coaching team and their expertise. In any sport, it is important to surround yourself with the right coaching team.

Now, not all sports are the same, but whatever sport you practice, if you want to excel, you need to have the right coach or coaches. Do you have the right coach? If not, what can you do to find the right one? One good way is to look at who coaches the best in your sport and age group. Then ask them if they would coach you too.

Chapter 5
Building a Support System

I won't predict anything historic. But nothing is impossible.
– Michael Phelps

www.FightingForGold.com

The third key to become a successful athlete is building a strong support system. This means having a group of people that help you reach your goals and objectives. My support system includes my family, my coaches, my teachers and my friends. I want to help you identify your support system. To do so, I will tell you what my support system does for me.

My family supports me by driving me to the rink five times a week, and sometimes more when I have weekend seminars or competitions. Usually my parents bring me, but sometimes, when my parents are not available, my grandparents will drive me to the rink. Also, when I have bad days at skating, my parents will not bring me down. They will always be happy for me because even if I make mistakes, they know I can build on them, and they always tell me I can do better next time. This is how my family is part of my support system.

My coaches support me by always pushing me to be my best. They want me to be consistent. My coaches say it is difficult to be consistent because I am still young. This means I have good days and I have bad days, and sometimes bad days become bad weeks. When I have a bad day, my coach will be harder on me because she knows I could be better. When I have a good day, my coach will allow me to practice more advanced jumps and spins, and that makes me feel happy and proud of myself. This is how my coaches are part of my support system.

My school is a student-athlete school. This means I go to school in the morning and I can skate in the afternoon every day from 1pm to 5pm. Not everyone in my school is an athlete so when I leave to go to skate, other students are in school learning. That means I miss class every afternoon. To get the information the other students got the previous afternoon, I go to school one hour before the other students so I can catch up with my teacher. This happens every morning. Sometimes I have to miss a school day for a competition or seminar. If I have an exam on that day, my teachers will allow me to take the exam during the next morning I am in school. This is how my teachers are part of my support system.

Now, because I skate so much, I do not have much time to see my friends. I cannot see them during the week because by the time I finish skating, I have to do my homework, eat supper and then it is bath and bed time. On the weekend, I have gymnastics because it helps me be more flexible, which will help my skating. This leaves Sunday to see my friends, but Sunday is usually family day. This makes it harder to even have friends, but I have three friends (and their parents) who understand that I have to work every day and even though I cannot see them a lot, it does not make me a bad friend. They are also always happy to see me when I'm available. So, they never complain that I cannot see them and that makes me really happy and I appreciate them very much for that. This is how my friends are part of my support system.

I hope that you now understand how to identify your support system. When you do find your support system, make sure you tell them how much you appreciate what they do for you.

Chapter 6
Sleeping Well

I've failed over and over and over again in my life
and that is why I succeed.
- Michael Jordan

Another important key to becoming a successful athlete is sleeping well. Sleeping well is very important for anyone, but especially for athletes. When you sleep, you are not just resting your body and rebuilding muscle, but you are also resting your brain and thoughts. A good sleep is important for your health. If you sleep well, you will be more resistant to colds and flus. It also improves your concentration, performance and mood, and helps with the ability to learn new tasks faster and better. Because you are more focused, sleep can also help prevent injuries. Most people need about 7 to 9 hours of sleep a night. As an athlete in training, you will probably need more than that. I sleep about 10 hours a night, which means I have to go to bed at 8:00pm because I have to wake up at 6:15am every morning to go to school.

When I first started the student-athlete program, I was going to bed too late and this had a negative impact on my skating. I was not doing well; I was tired and not giving my 100%. As of 2:00pm, I did not have the energy to push myself and did not have a good attitude. My coach told me that I had to go to bed earlier so that when I got to skating I would have the right amount of energy to stay focused. Since I changed my sleeping habit, I have improved a lot because I have the energy to skate after my day at school. I also have the right attitude on the ice. This means that when I do not get something right, I still have the right mindset to redo it until I get it right. Once I get it, I do it again until I can't get it wrong, which means I am consistent.

Chapter 7
Eating Well

Success consists of going from failure to failure without loss of enthusiasm.
– Winston Churchill

As an athlete, eating well is as much an important key to being a successful athlete as sleeping well. When you eat well it gives your body what it needs to stay healthy and full of energy, and have stronger muscles. When you eat junk all the time, your body is tired, and this can impact your performance. But what is junk food? It is chocolate, chips, candies, cookies, pizza, ice cream and my favorite, Nutella. I am not saying to never eat junk. I usually have a little, which is ok, but eating too much is not good for you. As a kid, I do enjoy eating junk food, but my parents usually say no. If your parents say no to eating junk food, do not get mad; it is because it is not good for you.

So what does eating well mean for me? It means eating fruits, vegetables, dairy, meat, fish, grains and nuts. It is also important to eat different colours of fruits and vegetables, as they each bring different nutrients to your body, including potassium, dietary fiber, folic acid, vitamin A, and vitamin C. I had the chance to attend different seminars that taught me about eating well. So even though I do not know what all these words mean, I know that my body needs them. My brother and I love fruits. If you put both cake and fruits in front of us, we would choose fruits. We even call my brother the fruit monster as he would eat fruits over dinner. My favorite fruits are strawberries, raspberries, blackberries, watermelon, pomegranate, cactus pear and kiwi. I like my vegetables both cooked and raw. My favorites are broccoli, orange peppers, carrots and, even though not considered a vegetable, tomatoes. I mostly eat my fruits and vegetables in my lunch and my skating snacks. Also, do not forget that choosing the right snacks is as important as your meals; you should pick fruits over cookies.

Every day I have to make sure I eat either chicken, meat, fish or eggs to get enough protein which my body needs to grow and develop. These foods also contain nutrients like iron, zinc, magnesium and vitamin B. My mommy is a vegetarian, so I also get to eat other types of proteins like beans and tofu, which I like too. My favorite protein is meat, but especially lamb chops. Dairy is also part of my diet, but I have an intolerance to lactose, which means I do not digest it well. I have to control how much dairy I eat, or eat lactose free products. Every day in my lunch or snacks, I have at least one portion of cheese and one of yogurt. I also drink milk with my breakfast. Another healthy way of eating is to introduce grains and nuts to your meals and snacks. Drinking water is also very important as it keeps your body hydrated.

I know you may not have enjoyed reading about eating and sleeping well, especially if you are young, but it really is important and is a necessary sacrifice to becoming a successful athlete, which brings us to the next chapter.

Chapter 8
Making Sacrifices

Develop success from failures. Discouragement and failure are two of the surest stepping stones to success.
– Dale Carnegie

The sixth key to being a successful athlete is making sacrifices. Sacrifices can mean letting go of different things. In my case, the most important thing I have to sacrifice is time. I will show you how sacrificing time affects others, such as family and friends.

To help you understand what I mean by sacrificing time, I want to show you what a typical day in my life is. I wake up at 6:15 am; I dress and eat breakfast really quickly because the bus picks me up at the corner at 6:59am. I get to school around 7:30am and class starts at 7:50am. I stay in school until 12:22pm. I get picked up at 12:22pm from school and get driven to the rink. I eat my lunch in the car because I have no time to eat at the rink. I get dropped off in front of the arena around 12:55pm and my skating lessons start at 1pm. I then have both on-ice and off-ice lessons until 5pm. I have two short breaks during that afternoon. That is when I eat my snacks, usually fruits or vegetables. I get picked up from the rink between 5:00pm and 5:40pm, and I am home between 5:45pm and 6:15pm. I then do my homework and when my mom arrives, around 6:30pm, I eat dinner. When I am finished eating, it is time to get ready for bed. I need to be in bed by 8:00pm so I can have enough rest to get through the following day. This is my routine from Monday to Friday, every week. This is what I mean by sacrificing time.

As you can see, because of my busy schedule, I do not get to see my family or friends very much. I basically only have weekends to see anyone, but I also need to rest on Sunday so I can be ready for the following week. I usually like to stay home on Sundays in my pyjamas, although I added singing lessons to my Sunday routine, just for fun. In fact, I only get to see my family and friends during special occasions, such as birthday parties. This is what I mean by sacrificing my family and friends. I am lucky that I have family and friends that understand that I have to work hard every day to reach my dreams.

Chapter 9
Having the Right Equipment

Success is where preparation and opportunity meet.
– Bobby Unser

www.FightingForGold.com

Another key to being a successful athlete is having the right equipment. Imagine a soccer player playing with running shoes instead of soccer cleats. Do you think that soccer players will be at their best playing with running shoes? Of course not! The same goes for all sports. Now, having the right equipment will not make you a successful athlete on its own, but it will help you perform and be at your best.

In my case, I need the following equipment. I need skates, skate guards, running shoes, proper clothing and a skating bag to carry all my equipment. I also keep exercise equipment in my bag such as a skipping rope, a spinner, training elastics, as well as a makeup kit required for competitions. Finally, I have to have the right dress for my competitions. I will discuss the two most important pieces of equipment, my skates and my dress.

Each skater has their own equipment based on their preferences and comfort. The most important piece of equipment is my skates. My skates need to be the perfect size, comfortable and have proper ankle support. If I do not have the right size, I can get really hurt and I do not want that. In order to purchase the right skate, I have to go to a store specialized in figure skating. I live in Montreal and the store I always go to is called "La Maison du Patin" because they always make sure I have the right skates. To do so, they not only measure my foot, but they ask me questions about what jumps and spins I am practicing to make sure I have the right boot and blade to support the impact on the ice. Blades are as important as the skating boot because they have different types and sizes of picks to help with specific jumps. Once I find the right boot and blade combination, they put my skates on and mold them to my feet. Because I have a narrow foot, I always prefer wearing the "Jackson" brand. They are great and super comfortable. I highly recommend them.

Another key piece of equipment is my competition outfit. When I started competing, my parents bought my first dress at the skating store off the rack. I like to have beautiful dresses with lots of sparkles and pretty colors. My first dress was icy blue like Queen Elsa from Frozen. Actually, my first solo song was from the same movie. You see, it is important that the dress fits well with the music I skate to. That was two years ago. My coach changed my solo and my song so I had to get a new dress to fit with the new song. The difference this time is I could not buy an off the rack dress. My coach says that at my level, I need to have a unique dress so I had my dress made. It is beautiful; coral with gold details, and very sparkly. I love to put on my competition dress because it makes me feel special and confident.

Now that I told you about the equipment I need to perform, what equipment do you think is important for your sport? Do you think you have the right equipment to be at your best? Remember, having the right equipment will not only help you perform better, but it can also help prevent injuries.

Chapter 10
Looking Up to Role Models

*I am building a fire, and every day I train, I add more fuel.
At just the right moment, I light the match.*
– Mia Hamm

www.FightingForGold.com

The eighth key to being a successful athlete is having one or more role models to look up to. A role model is a person looked to by others as an example to be imitated. In sports, a role model is usually someone who is the best or near the top of your sport. For example, if you are a hockey player, maybe a good role model is Sidney Crosby or Alex Ovechkin. If you are a soccer player, Lionel Messi or Cristiano Ronaldo may come to mind. The important thing is that you have someone to look up to as an example of what you would like to become in the future. Preferably, you want to become better. In my case, I have two role models for sports.

The first role model I have is Kaetlyn Osmond. She is a Canadian figure skater who won both an Olympic Bronze medal in 2018 in the ladies' singles event and Olympic gold as part of the Canadian team in the team event. I love watching her because she is an amazing performer. She has a great connection with the judges, the music and the crowd. She has a beautiful smile. These are all qualities that are important to becoming an elite figure skater and I look up to her for those abilities.

Another role model of mine is Alina Zagitova, a Russian figure skater. She won the Olympic Gold Medal in 2018 in the ladies' singles event. She is one of my role models because I like the way she is always consistent in her performance. Consistency is super important in figure skating because you only have one chance in a performance. You either get it right or you miss it. You cannot start over. Alina Zagitova rarely misses her elements in her performance, which is why she is one of the best figure skaters in the world. I definitely want to be more consistent going forward.

Now, I have told you about my role models relating to my sport. I also have a role model when it comes to other qualities that are not necessarily related to sports. Hard work is very important to success in anything you do in life. I am lucky to have a role model at home.

My mother is a role model to me because she works hard every day. Even when she comes home from work and is tired and would prefer sitting down, she makes supper, helps with my homework and puts my brother and me to bed. This "never stop" attitude is a quality that will be useful to me if I want to have a figure skating career.

I have shared with you my role models and I hope you now understand what a role model is and how important they are if you want to be a successful athlete. If you already have role models, great. If not, I encourage you to find one or more.

Chapter 11
Having the Right Mindset

Success is a state of mind. If you want success, start thinking of yourself as a success.
– Joyce Brothers

In any sport, you need to practice to get better and learn the techniques. If practicing is very important, a key to being a successful athlete is having the right mindset.

To be a successful athlete you need perseverance. When I am on the ice, I always give 100%, I never give up and I am a fighter. When I do not get something right, I continue doing it until I get it. How many times have I fallen? Too many to count, but I always got back up and tried again. Having that "never give up" attitude is a key to success for me. It is not just on the ice that I have to always give my best; it also important to give my best off the ice. Even though I am the youngest and smallest, I always work as hard, if not harder, in my off-ice trainings like cardio, stretching and muscle strength. I have to admit, stretching class is not my favorite and I have cried a few times. My daddy tells me that to reach my dreams, I have to work even harder on things I don't like as much.

As an athlete, you also need self-motivation. When I am on break, I actually continue working, stretching and warming up, which is important so that I don't get hurt. Sometimes that means continuing to work while others are talking, playing and having fun, but I do it because I want to be the best I can be. It does not matter what the others are doing; what matters is the effort I put in. I know that the effort I put in will reflect how I perform. My coach says that I am independent, which means I work hard even when she is not teaching me or looking.

To be successful, you also need to have a positive attitude. When things do not go your way, you cannot get upset because that will not help you perform. If you do, things will actually get worse. You need to always keep a positive attitude, which means believe that you are able to get it right, and work harder to actually get it right. When I am not performing well, instead of getting upset, I visualize what I have to do and set objectives for myself. That helps me break down the steps I need to do to improve my performance.

Even if skating is not a team sport, having good sportsmanship is also very important. Those are qualities I bring to my sport. That means that when my friends are doing well, I am happy for them and I am proud. I like seeing them succeed and achieve one of their objectives; it makes me very happy for them, even if they are competing against me. My skating friends also help me sometimes and cheer me up when I am having a bad day. I am always happy when they share tricks with me, and I am lucky to have them. It feels really good when they wish me luck before a competition, cheer for me and congratulate me after a competition. I do the same for them. Sometimes, I ask my parents to bring me to see a friend compete even if I am not competing that day. That is what I call sportsmanship in an individual sport.

Respect for those teaching me is also very important so I can get better. I have to listen to my coaches when they are teaching me skills and techniques because they have more experience than I do. I know that my success makes them happy and they want the best for me. They teach me the right techniques, and the steps of skating. It is like a recipe; you always have a first step to do, a second, a third and so on. It is important to do them all correctly and in order, and coaches make sure that you do. Respect is important, not just with those teaching you, but with everyone around you. You always need to show respect for others if you want to be respected yourself.

Another quality I bring to skating is confidence in my performance. When I am on the ice, I love to entertain. I connect with the music, the crowd and, if in a competition, with the judges. Every little detail in a performance counts: keeping up with the music, smiling, lifting my head, stretching my arms and legs, looking at the crowd with a little attitude. In skating, I also have to pay as much attention to the way I present myself, the dress I wear, the makeup I put on and how my hair is done. Attention to detail is a huge part of success, and the same will apply to your sport. Even if I do this well now, I still have a lot of improvement to do. Once you reach higher levels, most of your competitors will be able to perform, but what will push someone to the top is if they do the little things right.

So, do you have the right attitude? The right mindset to succeed? If so, continue to build on that. If not, I strongly suggest you make some changes. You will quickly see a positive change in your performance.

Chapter 12
Performing in School

If you tell the truth, you don't have to remember anything.
- Mark Twain

The tenth key to being a successful athlete is to perform well in school. Why write a chapter on the importance of good results in school? Why is school so important to an athlete? Because if you have good results in school, you can choose what you will be doing later in life. Although my dream is to be an Olympic gold medalist, I also want to be able to choose the career that I wish to have after skating. In addition, you never know if injury will prevent you from having a career in your sport and it is important to have what my parents call a plan B. I know I still have time to change my mind and I am still young, but if you ask me now, I wish to become an athletic therapist. Even if I know it means a lot of years in school, lots more homework and lessons.

So, to keep my grades up in school, I need to work as hard in the classroom as I do at the rink. It means putting in as much effort in my homework and lessons as I do on practicing my sport. It is not always easy because sometimes I am tired from practicing or I get home late because I practiced at night. For example, when I was not in a student-athlete program at school, I skated four nights during the school week so I had to do my homework when I got home, even though it was late. I also had to do school work during the weekend to catch up on what I did not have a chance to finish during the week. It is easier for me now because I can do my homework earlier since I skate during the day, which has been great for me.

Chapter 13
Where I Am Now

Gold medals aren't really made of gold. They're made of sweat, determination, and a hard-to-find alloy called guts.
— Dan Gable

www.FightingForGold.com

Now that I've told you about the 10 keys to success, I want to tell you where I am now in my short career.

I started competitive skating three and a half years ago. My first year, I was a little nervous and fell a lot. I knew I could be good, but I also knew I had to work hard to get better. Being on the ice, showing my solo and hearing the spectators clap was motivating. For the rest of the competition season, my goal was not to get a medal, but it was to improve every time I got on the ice. Improving made me happy and proud that all the hard work was paying off. At the end of each season, there is a provincial competition.

My first season, I finished 8th out of 19 skaters in the province. Although I did not win a medal in my first year, I really enjoyed the experience. I was really happy and I was looking forward to the next season. My first medal came only in my second season. The funny thing is I did not think I would win a medal so I just waited in the stands for my scoring sheet. Someone had to get me from the stands when they called my name for the medal ceremony. I was so surprised, but also happy and proud. So were my parents and my coach. That year I got a few more medals, and every time I felt satisfaction, and this pushed me to work even harder to continue to improve. At the end of my second season, in the provincial competition, I finished 6th.

In my third year, I started my competition season with not only a silver medal but five points over my highest score to date. I also finished my season ranked 3rd in the province while, once again, obtaining my highest point score ever at that time.

I am now in my fourth year of skating at a competitive level. My first competition of the season was amazing; I did really well and beat my highest score to date. I continued building on that throughout the season. At the provincial competition, I finished 3rd once again. Although I was very happy, I did not perform at my best and did not beat my highest score of the season. I let my stress take over and skated very cautiously. I also did not pay attention to what I was eating and I was sleeping later than usual. This had a negative impact on me. So, when I came back to practice to prepare for the last competition of the season, I worked with a more normal routine. I paid attention to what I was eating and when I was sleeping. It worked. During my competition, I was more confident than ever. It was the best one of the year, and my career. I beat my high score in terms of points and finished second in the province. It was more than I expected, and a great way to end the season.

Today, I am more motivated than ever before, and I will continue to put in the effort and the time to excel at my passion. I continue to work hard to improve and to realize my dream of being an Olympic figure skater.

About the Author

Emma Araish lives in Montreal, Canada.

Currently, Emma attends Wilfrid-Bastien School in the student-athlete program. She enjoys spending time with her family, reading and, of course, figure skating.

To order more books, please visit:
www.amazon.com or www.FightingForGold.com

Finally, if you have been inspired by this book, the best thing you can ever do is pass that on and be a wonderful role model for others. This world needs more shining lights.

www.ingramcontent.com/pod-product-compliance
Lightning Source LLC
LaVergne TN
LVHW051507070426
835507LV00022B/2970